Travel

Tips

By
Alison Tilley

Illustrations by
Graham Harrop

Published in 1996 by: Alison Tilley and Dan Hicks Productions

For more information contact:
Alison Tilley or Dan Hicks
39 Riviera Dr. Unit #3
Markham, Ontario
Canada L3R 8N4
1-800-569-7111
Fax: (416) 486-2454

Edited by: Margaret Hannan
Interior & Cover by: Willie Liang
Printed and bound in Canada

Canadian Cataloguing in Publication Data

Tilley, Alison, 1969 - Tilley travel tips

3rd ed.   ISBN 0-9697771-3-2

1. Travel - Handbooks, manuals, etc. I. Harrop, Graham II. Title.

G151.T56 1996   910'.2'02   C96-900850-3

PART I - PLAN AND PREPARE

PART II - THE TRIP

INTRODUCTION

As early as I can recall, I've been fascinated with exotic places. Travelling was a big part of my family life when I was growing up. We visited places like Guatemala and Belize, which were relatively untravelled by tourists at that time. There is no doubt my parents helped spark my curiosity and relentless desire to explore.

For me, travelling is inspiring, empowering, and fascinating—it gives me a breather in the whirlwind of everyday life. It has made me more aware and appreciative.

If you are a would-be wanderer who longs to travel, be it for a week, a month or a year, I hope these tips will be of help to you.

Alison Tilley

PART I

PLAN AND PREPARE

1

RESEARCH YOUR DESTINATION

◆ In order to get the most out of your travel experience, be sure to familiarize yourself thoroughly with your destination.

◆ Look at a map of the world and write a list of places you might like to visit. Write down what you want to do and see in each place.

◆ Visit your public library; browse through guide books; write to the tourist offices for each country that you plan to visit; contact auto clubs; search the Internet; talk to others who have visited the area; attend lectures and travel shows.

◆ When you request information, be specific.

◆ Your research should include: accommodation, weather, maps, up-to-date guide books,

tineraries, local timetables and events, airline, train, ferry, and cruise schedules.

▶ Even if you are not interested in guided tours, study the itineraries of different tour companies. They can be an invaluable help in designing your own schedule.

▶ Look for phrase books and begin learning basic words and phrases.

▶ Be realistic in your planning–be aware of your time restrictions and then prioritize your "must-do's" in order of priority.

▶ Book your trip!

2
FIRST THING FIRST

PASSPORT

◆ Applications for passports are available from government offices or local travel agencies. Processing time is about five working days.

◆ Many countries require that your passport be valid for at least six months even if you plan to visit for only a few days.

◆ If you plan extensive international travel, request a "business-size passport", which has extra pages for stamps and visas.

VISA

◆ Your travel agent or airline representative should know if the country which you are visiting requires a visa–a stamp in your passport permitting you to enter that country for a

ecific period. Some countries require you to
ave a visa, even if you are just passing through.

As some countries will withhold your pass-
ort until a visa has been issued, it is best to
btain your visa(s) before leaving home. Allow
ur to six weeks for processing.

Carry extra passport-size photographs in case
ou need to get a visa en route.

RIVING PERMIT

If you plan on driving abroad, consider get-
ng an International Driving Permit from your
cal automobile association.

EALTH RECORDS

Check with your local public health office at least
0 weeks before departure for information about
quired immunization. As some shots require
peat visits and can make you feel slightly ill, be
re to have them well in advance of your departure.

Carry updated medical records, noting immu-
izations, medications and allergies, as well as a copy
f your health insurance policy, your provincial

ealth card, and your health plan number.

• Have complete medical and dental examina-
ons before any long trip.

TRAVEL TICKETS

• Charging all airline tickets on a credit card
ould provide flight benefits. These could
iclude free flight insurance and frequent flyer
iileage points.

• Check your plane tickets carefully against the
etails on your itinerary to make sure there are
o errors.

• Enquire about departure fees from foreign
estinations.

• As a safety precaution, try to book all your
ansportation to ensure that you arrive at your
estinations during daylight hours.

• Photocopy your passport, visas, plane tickets,
redit cards, travellers' cheques, drug prescrip-
ons and other important documents. Carry
opies separately and leave a copy at home with
omeone you trust.

3
HEALTH TIPS

DDITIONAL PRE-TRIP
EALTH PLANNING

If you require medication, take enough to last
e whole trip, plus extra. Know generic names
d carry a prescription in case you have to buy
ore medicine while abroad.

Split medication into two containers. Keep
e in your carry-on luggage, in case your other
ggage goes astray.

If you wear eye glasses, take a spare pair with you.

If you carry a syringe, it's wise to have an
ficial letter from a doctor to avoid problems at
stoms' inspections.

Take a first aid kit.

♦ Travelling non-stop can be tiring; build in some rest days to give yourself time to recharge.

HEALTH INSURANCE COVERAGE

♦ Make sure that the type of travel insurance you purchase covers all your planned activities, e.g., scuba diving, snorkeling, hiking, kayaking.

♦ Can foreign hospitals and clinics bill directly to the insurance company?

♦ Can you extend the time of your coverage while away?

♦ Are all emergency flights covered?

♦ Check whether or not your insurer has a 24-hour toll-free number in each of the countries in which you are travelling. If not, can you call them collect?

♦ Consider becoming a member of the International Association for Medical Assistance to Travellers (IAMAT). Membership includes a booklet listing English-speaking doctors in 120 countries around the world. In Canada phone (519) 836-0102. In the United States phone (716) 754-4883.

4
MONEY MATTERS

• Carry a combination of travellers' cheques, cash and credit cards.

• Always check in advance about the refund policy for lost or stolen travellers' cheques.

• Write down the serial numbers of your travellers' cheques and keep the list in a different place from your cheques. Your record of the numbers may speed up any claim for reimbursement.

• Carry your money with you at all times, but not all in the same pocket or money belt.

• Take 20% more money than you think you'll need.

• Take $40 US in one-dollar bills for tips and cab fares.

Take two widely used credit card such as American Express, Visa or MasterCard. Check the expiry dates and credit limits.

Try to start out with a small amount of cash (the equivalent of $50) in the currency of the country you'll be visiting. This should be enough for taxis, tips or small necessities on arrival.

Take a moment to estimate how much you should pay, or receive, before making any money transaction. When changing travellers' cheques, watch the teller count the money in front of you, then count it back carefully in front of him, or her.

Before you go, get the fax number of your bank and the manager's name. If you need more money while abroad, fax him/her to send you a draft. Specify the city you're in, the bank, and the exact address.

Carry some personal cheques, otherwise, you may have trouble buying travellers' cheques or getting a cash advance.

ANSWERING MACHINE MESSAGES
BURGLARS LOVE MOST..

5

KEEPING YOUR HOME SAFE

MAKE YOUR HOME
APPEAR OCCUPIED

To make sure that your home is safe before you go away, it should look as if you were still there.

• To try to eliminate a hiding place for burglars, have your shrubbery trimmed to a height below the first floor window sills.

• Encourage neighbours to use your driveway for parking.

• Use automatic timers that turn lights and radios on and off. Set your radio dial to a talk show station as voices will help to deter burglars. Stagger times for the lights to go on and off in different rooms.

• Arrange to have your lawn mowed or snow shovelled.

• Be sure the message on your answering machine does not imply that your house is vacant.

• Arrange for some garbage and trash to be put out for pickup as usual.

CONTINUE YOUR SERVICES

• Have a neighbour or friend collect your mail. Having it held at the post office can alert postal employees that your house is empty.

• Stop newspaper delivery. Do not give a time limit.

• Pay bills that will be due in your absence, and arrange for the payment of others that may arrive while you're away.

BURGLAR DETERRENTS

• Place Neighborhood Watch and security systems decals on windows at the front and back of

he house. These decals are a proven deterrent
o burglary.

▶ Arrange for secure storage of furs, jewelry, and
ther valuables outside the house while you are
way.

▶ About 80% of the stolen property recovered
y police cannot be identified. To make sure
ou can identify your property, use an electric
ngraving pencil (which police may lend you),
nd inscribe your driver's license or social insur-
nce number on valuables. On the outside
oors, post notices that your valuables have been
narked for identification.

▶ Have your alarm system checked before
eparture.

▶ On the exterior doors of your house, place
otices listing the phone number of someone,
ther than yourself, who can be contacted if the
larm is set off. When police respond, the alarm
vill have to be deactivated and reset, otherwise,
 smart burglar could set off the alarm, vanish,
hen re-visit later.

◆ Provide sufficient lighting at all doors and windows.

◆ Install motion detectors which, when activated, illuminate the outside of your home.

◆ Light all gates and fences surrounding your property.

◆ Leave some lights burning all night.

OTHER PRECAUTIONS

◆ Leave an itinerary with someone, so that you can be notified in case of an emergency.

◆ Leave a door key and a key to the burglar alarm system (if you have one) with a trusted neighbour.

◆ Inform the police, the fire department and your neighbours when you install a local alarm.

◆ Tell your neighbours what sounds to expect.

◆ Ask them to call the police if the alarm is activated.

HOME INSURANCE COVERAGE

▸ Ask your insurance agent about home checks while your home in unoccupied. You may not e covered if your home has not been visited at egular intervals, while you are away.

▸ Ask your insurance representative to provide ou with a home owner's inventory checklist.

▸ Conduct a personal property inventory to elp determine how much insurance you should arry. This could save thousands of dollars in ase of fire or theft.

▸ Consider videotaping and photographing in olour, the exterior, interior, and contents of our home. Store them with a trusted friend or eighbour or leave them in a safety deposit box.

6
TAKING THE RIGHT GEAR

There are many travel cases available. Be sure to select the right one to suit your needs. Much will depend on the age and strength of the user.

◆ Suitcases and duffel bags are not practical if you'll be moving about a lot. Consider buying a travel pack which is a combination backpack, shoulder bag and a suitcase. It has a shoulder strap which can zip inside the pack and a handle in the middle. It looks more like a big bag than a backpack, holds a lot, and is much easier to carry than most duffel bags or suitcases. Another advantage of using a travel pack is that your hands are free. Get a good quality one with internal metal frames.

◆ If you prefer a large suitcase, consider one with sturdy wheels that are replaceable (they

hay wear down), and pivot for turns in eleva-
ors, or use a portable, folding, carry cart.

Zippered side pockets provide useful extra
pace, but avoid placing valuables in them as
hey're obvious targets for light-fingered folks.

7

PACKING TIPS

◆ Over-packing can seriously ruin a trip. "Travel light, travel happy." (Take half the clothes; twice the money!)

◆ Choose what you'd like to take and then eliminate all non-essentials. Take only what you can carry.

◆ Look for lightweight, easy-to-care-for, hand-washable clothing. Test each item for comfort by sitting, squatting, and kneeling when buying. Try to co-ordinate separates which will combine to make various "outfits".

◆ To show respect for other cultures, consider the customs of the country you are visiting and dress accordingly.

• Select a basic shoe that's suitable for both day and evening wear. Never take new shoes on a trip.

• Pack shoes in a breathable cloth bag. Baking soda in exercise shoes helps control odor.

• When buying hiking boots, buy at least a half a size too big. This prevents black–and–blue toenails when going down steep hills.

WE GOT EVERYTHING IN ONE CASE...

CHECK-IN

• Photocopy and take only essential pages from guide books. Use both sides of the paper to save space.

• Pack those items you dare not lose (medications, toiletries, camera, etc.) in your carry-on bag in case your luggage goes astray.

8
WHAT TO PACK

The secret to keeping it light is to make a list. Include as many multi-purpose items as possible. Always select a wardrobe that will match the climate of the countries you plan to visit.

Things To Consider Packing For Warm Weather Trips

◆ a hat

◆ 2 pairs of long shorts

◆ 3 shirts

◆ comfortable sandals which can be worn with everything

◆ water-repellent, hooded, windbreaker

◆ running shoes

◆ rubber thongs for the beach, or shower

- 2 bathing suits

- a sarong, a piece of fabric roughly 3 feet by 6 feet—makes an excellent beach towel, skirt and cover up.

- socks and underwear

- a light sweater

- camera, case, film and lens cleaner

- sunglasses, neck cord, case and cleaning cloth

- beach bag

- mask and snorkel

- sun block with an SPF of at least 15

- travel alarm clock

- a pocket currency conversion calculator

- a small pocket flashlight

- a small, inflatable neck pillow—useful for long plane flights!

- first aid kit

◆ bug repellent and mosquito net (for countries where malaria is prevalent)

◆ biodegradable laundry soap

◆ pen, paper, small notebook

◆ a couple of good paperback books

◆ a spoon and Swiss army knife

◆ a pair of scissors

◆ a mini sewing kit

◆ facial or toilet tissue

◆ a small sturdy day pack

◆ face cloth

◆ sink stopper

◆ dental floss

◆ If you pack an electric razor, hairdryer or computer, you will need both a voltage converter and a wall-plug adapter for them to function outside of North America. An extension cord would also be useful.

PART II

THE TRIP

9

BAGGAGE TIPS

Here's what you can do to help ensure that your baggage doesn't go astray.

➤ Remove all old airline tags not related to your immediate travel.

➤ Remove hand-straps before placing luggage on conveyor belt.

➤ Attach tag both inside and outside your bag with your name, your business address, and your complete phone number. Avoid using your home address.

➤ Make sure the check-in agent puts a correctly coded destination tag on each one of your bags.

➤ Select luggage with combination locks, or buy

small padlock and lock the zippers shut. Have our partner carry a spare key.

If you're concerned that your baggage may not make the connecting flight, ask the ticket counter agent for "door storage," which means your bags will be last on and first off.

Try to make your bag distinguishable from others by using brightly coloured ribbons or tape.

Claim your luggage as soon as possible. Examine all luggage as it comes off the carousel. Report immediately to the airline's baggage representative if your luggage is damaged or missing.

For insurance purposes, list the contents of your bag.

10
FLYING TIPS

TO MAKE FLYING MORE PLEASANT:

▶ Arrive at the airport in plenty of time to obtain your seating preference.

▶ If you have long legs, ask to sit in the front row or beside the emergency exit.

▶ Drink plenty of water before and during your flight to prevent dehydration.

▶ Take eye drops and remove contact lenses in flight. The dry cabin air may cause sore eyes.

▶ Wear loose clothing with an expandable waistband because your body may swell during a flight.

▶ Take a jacket or sweater because cabin air temperature may fluctuate.

• Avoid alcohol and caffeine as they cause dehydration and can disrupt your sleep pattern.

• Try to eat, stay awake, and sleep, according to changes in your time schedule during the flight, and immediately after arrival.

• Try to have pre-arranged accommodation for the first two nights. After a long flight this will help to minimize stress and recover from jet lag. It takes about two days to adjust and relax into your new time zone.

• Allow enough time between flights to clear customs, or to get your luggage transferred to another carrier.

COMFORTABLE...?

11

TRAVELLERS' CHEQUES

◆ Expect to pay a 1% service charge to cash travellers' cheques at exchange offices. A bank or a credit card company often won't charge yo The worst exchange rates are found at borders, railway and airport exchange offices, hotels, anc restaurants.

◆ Buy most of your travellers' cheques in denominations of hundreds and fifties, with about $200 in twenties and tens. You may war to change a small cheque to get you through th last few hours of your trip.

◆ Be prepared to present your passport when changing travellers' cheques abroad. (Be sure to put it back immediately into your security pock or money belt.)

In some foreign countries, you can't convert the local currency back into dollars when you leave. If so, pay for purchases with small bills, or consider using your credit card.

Save the receipts from all the money you change. When you are departing, many countries require that you show these receipts if you want to convert local currency back into U.S. dollars.

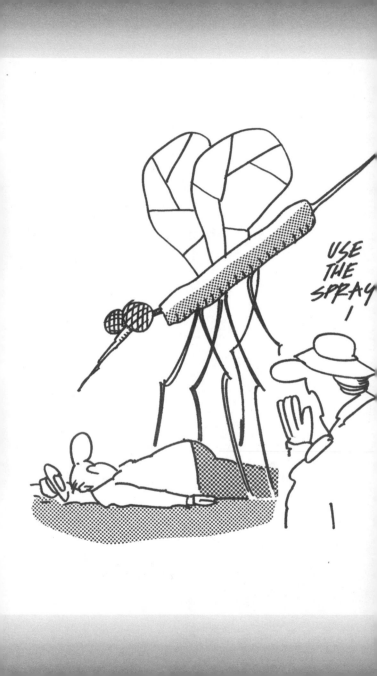

12

HEALTH TIPS

EALTH TIPS WHILE TRAVELLING

 happy traveller must be a healthy traveller.
o avoid unnecessary ailments consider the
llowing:

OOD AND WATER

• Avoid drinking tap water (including ice cubes)
nless you're sure of its source. Bottled water is
fest. Be sure to break the seal yourself.

• Keep a bottle of water in your bathroom to
rush your teeth.

• If you are suspect about the safety of the
rinking water, rinse off silverware and glasses
ith bottled water before using them.

• By eating hot food (heat kills bacteria) you
ay avoid intestinal distress.

◆ Eat at well-known and busy restaurants that look clean and well-run.

OTHER TIPS WHILE TRAVELLING

◆ Pharmacist are usually very knowledgeable about local health problems and health services. They can recommend local doctors and/or render first aid.

◆ Use a sun block with an SPF rating of 15 or more and apply it to all exposed skin. Wear a hat, sunglasses and closely woven clothing.

In tropical or wilderness locations, shake out our shoes before putting them on, as precaution ainst scorpions and other "nasties".

Your best prevention against being bitten by osquitoes, which can carry malaria is to:

-Wear a loose, long-sleeved shirt, long pants and socks.

-Use an insect repellent.

-Avoid wearing perfume, scented deodorant or hair sprays.

-Sleep under a mosquito net or a ceiling fan.

Fever and headaches which occur even two ars after travelling in a malarious region war- nt a malaria check from your doctor.

In developing countries, avoid eating fresh sal- ls as they may be washed in questionable water. it isn't cooked and can't be peeled, don't eat it!

To prevent ear infections after swimming in e ocean, rinse out your ears with bottled water.

13

HOTEL TIPS

OTEL SAFETY

Know the location of the two exits nearest our room and know how to find the door and nlock it, in the dark.

Know where the fire alarm on your floor is.

Read and memorize all safety measures, in case emergency.

In a hotel, lock the balcony doors and any indows accessible from outside.

OOKING YOUR ROOM

When you make a hotel reservation, guarantee our room by sending a deposit.

Be sure to ask for any available discounts or

ograades. For example, corporate, seniors, CAA,
AAA and off-season rates.

Smoke-free rooms are available in many
hotels. If you want one, just ask.

Call to confirm your reservation if delayed.

Ask to see rooms on different floors so you
can compare and choose. Look at the view,
check the door and window locks (and air con-
ditioner, if there is one) to make sure they work;
pull back the bed covers to make sure the sheets
are fresh; flush the toilet; turn on the shower to
make sure it runs; and listen to the traffic noise.

Stay at hotels with smoke detectors and automatic sprinklers.

If you need to stay another night at your
hotel but they are sold out, try again at 6:01 PM.
Rooms that were not guaranteed with a credit
card are then made available and you may get
lucky.

If you have several charges on a hotel bill, ask

r your bill the night before you leave. This gives
ou the time to check the charges, and to have
ny corrections made before your departure.

• Use traveller's checks or credit cards, rather
an carrying large amounts of cash.

14

SAFETY TIPS

PERSONAL SAFETY

Consider taking a self-defense course to learn physical, verbal and mental techniques to protect yourself.

Always trust your instincts. If something doesn't feel right, it probably isn't.

Shout "FIRE" or "POLICE"; people are more apt to help you if they think they're safe.

Be careful to cover the number on your telephone calling card in hotels and at airports in case thieves are watching. Avoid saying the number out loud.

Book a hotel room in the center of town where you can walk to shops, restaurants and sights.

- Take an organized city tour either by day or by night.

- Dress so that you do not draw undue attention to yourself, nor do you show lack of respect for local customs and culture.

- Ignore annoying overtures from men/women.

- Never hitchhike and never pick up hitchhikers.

- Don't walk through alleys. Stick to well-lit areas.

- Avoid advertising your wealth. Keep expensive cameras hidden in a small day-pack and leave costly jewelry and watches safely at home.

- Remain alert to what's happening around you. Be aware of loud arguments, bumps and other incidents, which may be staged to distract you while someone else steals your wallet or handbag.

- Be especially careful at buses, train stations, airports, outdoor festivals, subways and other crowded places; these are all popular with pickpockets.

◆ If you do fall victim to crime, remember, you embassy is there to help.

◆ Select a secure, well-lit parking spot, especiall if your shopping is likely to extend through sun down.

◆ Lock all doors when exiting your vehicle. If in an attended garage, only leave your ignition key with the attendant.

◆ Do not walk alone in a parking lot, especially at night. If you are alone, or feel uncomfortable ask a guard to escort you.

◆ Check your back seat before getting in your vehicle, and then lock all doors.

◆ If approached by a robber, co-operate, remain calm and surrender your valuables.

◆ When using public transportation, sit near a companion or the driver.

◆ Walk on the side of the street facing oncoming traffic.

Be suspicious if a friendly traveller at the airport asks you to check-in one of his suitcases claiming he or she doesn't want to pay excess luggage charges. The luggage could be lined with drugs and you could find yourself in prison.

Unless there's a meter, make sure a reasonable fare is established before you get into a taxi cab. Get advice on reasonable rates from the staff at your hotel.)

HOTEL SAFETY

The most important possessions you need to protect are your passport, travellers' cheques, money, credit cards and airline tickets. Carry these items with you at all times or keep them in a secure place like secret pockets, a money belt or a hotel safe.

Put combination locks, padlocks or cable locks on all luggage.

Rental cars are natural targets for thieves, so do not leave possessions in an unattended car.

◆ Each night, empty the glove compartment in your car and keep it open so thieves can see that there is nothing to steal.

◆ Don't carry cash while shopping, if it can be avoided.

◆ When checking into hotels, insist on a room with a dead bolt and a peephole.

◆ Have a bellhop accompany you to your room to ensure that it is not occupied. Do this when you are first checking in and also when returning late at night.

◆ Tell the front desk clerk and switchboard not to give out your room number under any circumstance, but to take messages for you.

◆ Don't display the "Please make up the room" tag on your door, as it lets people know the room is unoccupied.

◆ Use a sealed envelope to keep credit cards and money in your hotel's safe.

◆ Females should check into hotels as Mrs., not Ms. Consider wearing a wedding ring if you are not married.

◆ Don't advertise the fact that you are alone

◆ Don't leave your room key at the front desk of your hotel as it may be "borrowed" and your room robbed before you return.

15
PHOTO TIPS

Film can be very expensive abroad, so pack more than you think you'll need. Extra batteries are also advisable.

▶ As developing standards differ from country to country, it is best to develop your film at home.

▶ Ask, with at least a gesture, before taking a stranger's photograph, as camera customs vary in each country. Ask at your hotel if any photo restrictions should be noted.

▶ Tape your business card to the inside of your camera case and to your camera.

▶ Take photos in the early morning, or late afternoon, for the best lighting conditions.

▶ To avoid facial shadows and give more punch to pictures, use a flash when photographing people.

◆ Get the names and addresses of people you've captured on film and mail copies of photos to them. They'll be delighted! Taking two shots (one to keep; one to give away) is less expensive than having duplicate prints made.

◆ It's often more interesting to have people in photos instead of just scenery so try to include yourself in as many pictures as possible. You'll appreciate it later.

◆ Plan your shots; decide exactly what you want in each frame before you click that shutter!

◆ Avoid direct shots into the sun as this may damage the sensitive light meter in your camera. Shooting away from the sun results in the most pleasing effects.

◆ Look at postcards in hotel lobbies or shops, to find out where the best picture-taking spots and the nicest beaches are.

◆ Generally, security x-ray machines will not harm film with speeds up to 1000 ASA. If in doubt, have security hand-check your film.

16
A LITTLE EXTRA

▶ Send postcards home to yourself with suggestions for future trips. A daily postcard to yourself can also serve as your trip record–a real bonus if your photography fails.

▶ Take a small, lightweight address book for all the postcards you'll be sending, and to write down the names of the new friends you'll be meeting.

▶ Keep in touch with those you meet while travelling; their friendship will enrich later visits.

▶ In countries where you don't speak the language, ask your hotel clerk to give you a hotel business card with the name and address on it. Keep the card with you to show to taxi drivers.

◆ When visiting a city in a foreign country for the first time, take a bus tour. You'll see the major points of interest and you'll know where to return later.

◆ The hotel concierge is generally an all-knowing person who can provide indispensable information to a guest. He or she can help arrange everything from wake-up calls, tickets to the ballet, the circus, train reservations, a morning newspaper, postage, and even recommend where to shop and dine. Compensate him or her upon your departure for their assistance.

◆ Although widespread, tipping is not universal. Find out the local custom and respect it.

NOTES

NOTES

NOTES

NOTES